Let's Read About Pets

Puppies

JoAnn Early Macken

Reading consultant: Susan Nations

W

FRANKLIN WATTS

LONDON•SYDNEY

First UK hardback edition 2004
First UK paperback edition 2005

Franklin Watts
96 Leonard Street
London EC2A 4XD

Franklin Watts Australia
45-51 Huntley Street
Alexandria
NSW 2015

ISBN 0 7496 5761 8 (hardback)
ISBN 0 7496 5828 2 (paperback)

Published in association with Weekly Reader Early Learning Library, Milwaukee.

Printed in Hong Kong, China

Contents

Opening their eyes

A newborn puppy cannot see. Puppies open their eyes when they are about ten days old.

Can puppies hear?
A newborn puppy cannot hear. When they are older, puppies can hear much better than we can.

Using their noses

Puppies can smell very well. They sniff the air to learn about things. They sniff the ground, each other and you.

Long or short hair?

Puppies may have long hair or short hair. Puppies with long hair must be brushed more often. Some puppies need to be clipped.

Feeling happy or sad
A playful puppy wags its tail. A puppy may whine if it is lonely or scared. It may bark as a greeting.

Growling

Puppies may growl as a warning to you or other dogs. They sometimes also growl when they play.

Teeth

A puppy has baby teeth that fall out when its adult teeth grow through.
A puppy needs toys to chew on.

Eating and drinking

Be careful! Puppies will eat almost anything. Give your puppy fresh food and water every day.

Choosing a puppy

Pick a puppy that suits you. Some puppies like to relax. Others like to run all day. What do you like to do?

New words

clipped — when hair is cut

growl — a deep sound made by an angry dog

relax — to stay quiet and not rush around

sniff — to smell something

whine — a high crying sound

How to find out more

Here are some useful websites about puppies and dogs:

www.pdsa.org.uk
Click on "You and your pet" and then click on "Puppies and Dogs". Useful information on choosing a puppy, looking after your puppy and avoiding doggy dangers

http://aolsvc.petplace.aol.com
Click on "Dogs" in Pet Centers. Then click on Featured Articles "Just for Kids" for information about exercising your puppy, caring for its teeth and potty training

www.kidsseek.com.au
Click on "Your Family Pets", then "Dogs". Lots of useful information and links to websites around the world

Note We strongly advise that Internet access is supervised by a responsible adult.

Index

Notes for teachers and parents

This book is specially designed to support the young reader in the reading process. The familiar topic is appealing to young children and invites them to read — and re-read — the book again and again.
The full-colour photographs and enhanced text help the child during the reading process. After children develop fluency with the text and content, the book can be read independently.